Dad'Scool Carpool

180 unbearable but
good dad rhymes and jokes to
start your kids' school day and
hopefully, life off right

DAD BRAD BEHLE

ILLUSTRATED BY SOLEE AND PRESLEE BEHLE

INTRO

Ever since my oldest started school 10 years ago, I've tried to make the carpool commute more than a hurry, get in line, yell at bad drivers, only to leave my kids stressed, as they run to class and begin their day on the wrong foot.

What started out as listening to inspiring YouTube videos has morphed into what we call "quote and a joke." Each day, one of the kids oversees finding and sharing one of each. This has become my favorite time of the day. I cherish our mornings together.

Several years back, I took a new job. In the interview, I let them know how important the morning carpool was to me and that this time with my kids was non-negotiable, and truly a deal breaker for me accepting the job or not. I'm glad I planted my flag there. Jobs come and go, memories with my kids are forever.

We all have busy lives. It can be hard to find quality family time. In our carpool we joke, laugh, share uplifting quotes, talk about crushes, friend drama, recess plans, how school is going, what classes they like/are struggling with, and overall, just spend quality time together.

After 10+ years of doing this, I decided to make it easier for others and complied a resource to share meaningful bad rhymes and terrible dad jokes. I'm proud of my girls for their fun illustrations. You might not happen to agree with everything inside, but you can use this as time to discuss, smile, and laugh with your kids. Start the day off right.

My parents told me not to blink when my oldest was born because the time goes fast. That didn't make sense the first several years with the sleep deprivation, diaper changing and adjusting to new parent life. My oldest just turned 13. We have five more years with him in the house and his siblings aren't far behind.
Time does go fast.

I hope I can teach my kids a thing or two about a good life just as my parents have taught me. I sincerely hope this book helps you do the same with your kids. Because the truth is, the time with them matters. Make it quality. Our role as a mother and father is as important now as it ever has been.

I would love to hear some of your own Dad'Scool carpool stories.
Email brad@behlebranding.com.

DEDICATION

To Bode, Solee, Preslee and Hoven,

*I am grateful **to rise** each day as your dad. Your future is bright. Love you.*

To all the dads, moms and others that have stepped into these roles. Keep at it, keep trying your best. What you do matters. It might seem to go unnoticed at times, but you matter.

Dad'scool RHYME 1

We had a great summer with tons of fun,
Soaking up friendships in the warmth of the sun.
Kind of a bummer that it's all done,
But before you know it, a new summer will come.
Until then, lots to accomplish and so much to learn.
Then, it'll be time for another sun burn.
Wake each day and live like it's your last,
Strive to be better, be who you're meant to be,
A go getter and a giver.
You're loved by many and will do great things.
Oh, and please remember the sunscreen.
-Dad Brad

DAD JOKE 1

Do you know where I store all my dad jokes?

In a Dad-a-base.

A new school year is here
There's nothing to fear.
You'll learn, you'll play, have fun.
No matter what may come, you're awesome.
Now, go kick learning's bum.
-Dad Brad

DAD JOKE 2

-Mother:
"What did you learn at school today?"

Child:
"Not enough, I have to go back tomorrow!"

Dad'scool RHYME 3

It's a new day.
Be kind to others in all you do and say.
It'll come back to you in a big way.
Make yourself and others smile
It's the best payday.
-Dad Brad

DAD JOKE 3

-Knock, Knock:

Who's there?

A broken pencil

A broken pencil who?

Never mind. It's pointless.

Dad'scool RHYME 4

Plant a tree and like a tree, be.
They clean the air, filter water,
Provide shade and much more.
Each spring they turn a new leaf around.
They stand tall and are
Deeply rooted into the ground.
-Dad Brad

DAD JOKE 4

*Did you hear about the man who got
hit by the same bike every day?*

It was a vicious cycle.

Dad'Scool RHYME 5

DAD JOKE 5

My uncle's dogs are named, Rolex and Timex.

They're his watch dogs.

Dad's<u>cool</u> RHYME 6

I sure love taking you to school
Even with all the carpool fools.
I suppose they're trying their best,
Even though their driving manners
Should be put to rest.
How'd some even pass the driving test?
Some cars don't pull up far enough.
I guess they don't want their kids
To walk an extra step.
In life, it's that extra step that counts,
It'll stretch you and you'll grow, this, I know.
Sometimes it's easier said than done.
Now, go, there's the bell.
Hurry, Run!
-Dad Brad

DAD JOKE 6

What do you call a hen that counts its eggs?

A mathmachicken.

Dad'Scool RHYME 7

It's a great day, get on your way.
Be happy, be kind, work hard.
Great day on 3.

1,2,3, Great day!
-Dad Brad

1,2,3,
Great
day

DAD JOKE 7

Why did the M&M go to school?

It really wanted to be a smartie.

Quitters quit, and winners win,
Really, just try your best, above the rest.
This is the recipe for the ultimate winning test.
-Dad Brad

DAD JOKE 8

Why aren't clocks allowed in the library?

Because they tock too much.

Dad'Scool RHYME 9

I'm grateful for this morning and all the good in my life.
You're a blessing I'm blessed with, remember this.
Forever you, I'll cherish.
-Dad Brad

DAD JOKE 9

Do you wanna box for your leftovers?

No, but I'll wrestle you for them.

Big day ahead, go take advantage.
The goal is to feel accomplished at days end,
When you lay down your sweet head.
Be well rested for the day to start again.
-Dad Brad

DAD JOKE 10

What did the faster tomato say to the
other one during a race?

Ketchup.

Dad'Scool RHYME 11

DAD JOKE 11

What do you call an alligator in a vest?

An investi-gator.

 RHYME 12

Sing out loud, be happy, and dance.
Help yourself by helping others with every chance.
Doing this will give you a glance
Of a life with purpose, one that's enhanced.
-Dad Brad

DAD JOKE 12

How do athletes stay cool?

They have many fans.

# Dad'Scool RHYME 13

I'm tired, you're tired, it happens somedays.
Push through it, you'll get through it,
You'll be better off for it.
-Dad Brad

DAD JOKE 13

What did one hat say to the other?

You stay here, I'll go on ahead.

Dad'scool RHYME 14

It's fun to be kind, to yourself and to others.
Kind to your parents, your sisters, and brothers.
Kind to your friends, strangers, and peers.
Kind to all, especially the person in the mirror.
Being kind to all, is simply the best kind of kind.
-Dad Brad

DAD JOKE 14

What did the traffic light say to the other?

Don't look now, I'm about to change.

Dad'Scool RHYME 15

Take care of your health,
It's the ultimate wealth.
Go run, skip, and jump.
Be careless.
I think adults need a work recess.
Being a kid is truly the best.
-Dad Brad

DAD JOKE 15

What do you call a bear with no teeth?

A gummy bear.

Hey there kiddos,
It's a brand-new day.
Get on with it, do good in it,
That's how you win today.
-Dad Brad

New Day

DAD JOKE 16

Mickey Mouse:
"Doc, my knee hurts."

Doctor:
"Which Knee?"

Mickey:
"Disney."

Dad'Scool RHYME 17

No matter what you know,
There's still a ton to learn and grow.
Always strive to learn something new.
Growing and learning is fun to do.
-Dad Brad

DAD JOKE 17

I asked my dog, "What's five minus five?"

She said nothing.

I like to win; being competitive is fun.
In all you do, strive to be YOUR #1.
It won't always work out and that's okay.
It's the striving and trying that makes a winning day.
-Dad Brad

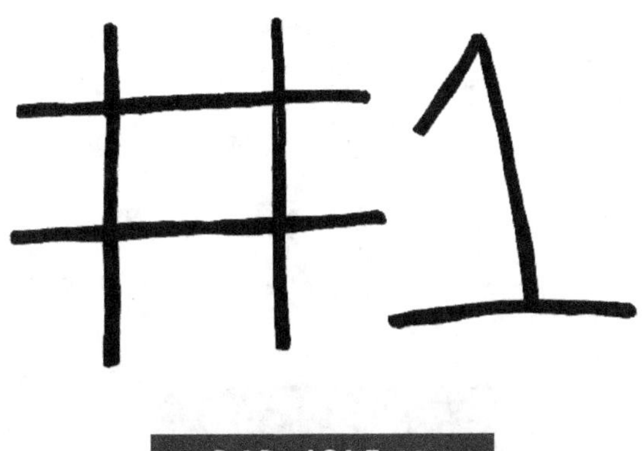

DAD JOKE 18

I heard in some parts of the world; people eat snails.

I guess they don't like fast food.

Dad'Scool RHYME 19

Sometimes in life you won't get along with others.
They were raised with different fathers and mothers.
Find it in your heart to still be kind,
Cause we're all brothers and sisters of humankind.
-Dad Brad

DAD JOKE 19

What is a cheerleader's favorite kind of cereal?

Cheerios.

 RHYME 20

I think as your parent, it's important to say,
To stand up for yourself in many ways.
Be bold in your answers that the teacher might ask,
Be confident that you can accomplish the task.
If others are rude to you, what can you do?
Be nice to you, it's the best thing to do.
Remember you're awesome. Yep, that's you.
-Dad Brad

DAD JOKE 20

Have you ever tried to eat a clock?

It's time consuming.

You're one of the lucky ones that woke up today.
There are people whose last day was yesterday.
So, let's do this; let's go, let's have a wonderful day.
Make it count, be happy, be grateful for today.
-Dad Brad

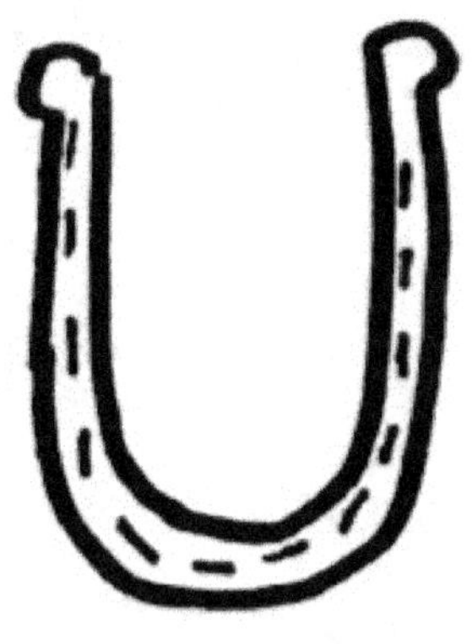

DAD JOKE 21

Why don't comedians tell jokes about boxing?

It's too difficult to come up with a punchline.

 RHYME 22

Set your alarm each day on your favorite number.
When it buzzes,
Say in your head something you're grateful for.
This will do wonders for your mind and much more.
-Dad Brad

DAD JOKE 22

What do you call a boomerang that won't come back?

A Stick.

Dad'scool RHYME 23

Hey, it's a new day, what do you say,
Get on your way, come what may,
You choose your attitude, today.
-Dad Brad

DAD JOKE 23

Why should you always knock on a refrigerator door before opening it?

In case there's a salad dressing.

At the days end, happy is how you want to be.
Do this by working hard, playing harder
And helping others, and you'll sleep joyfully.
-Dad Brad

WORK hard
play hard
Give back

DAD JOKE 24

What did the buffalo say when his son left for college?

Bison.

RHYME 25

Good morning, kids, we're off to school.
Learning and growing to avoid being a fool.
You know what you are? You're cool.
I'm glad you're part of our Dad'Scool carpool.
-Dad Brad

DAD JOKE 25

What's a snake's favorite subject in school?

Hisssssssstory.

Don't bottle up what's bugging you.
Talk to a parent, your teacher, your friend, too.
We all have bad moments, things we hide.
They fester and grow when you keep them inside.
Get them from the basement hiding in the dark.
Bring them out in the open and light the spark,
That'll dim the darkness and shine a new light.
Just keep going, it'll all be alright.
-Dad Brad

DAD JOKE 26

What did the horse say when it fell?

Help, I've fallen, and I can't giddy up.

Some days are lame.
It's part of the game.
The trick is for tomorrow
To not be the same.
-Dad Brad

DAD JOKE 27

What do you call a can opener that doesn't work?

A can't opener!

Dad'Scool RHYME 28

DAD JOKE 28

Dear Math,

Grow up and solve your own problems.

Dad'scool RHYME 29

Kind, not weak is what to strive for.
Treat others well and yourself even more.
Turn a cheek if someone is mean,
Walk away with high self-esteem.
But if it continues and they're not backing off
Sometimes it takes being more than soft.
There will always be bullies in school and life,
Standing up for yourself and others, is right.
So be kind, but not weak in all you do.
Stand up for others and stand up for you.
-Dad Brad

DAD JOKE 29

Why don't eggs tell jokes?

They'd crack each other up.

Not everything is forever
Some things go away.
Take advantage of each day,
Cause some things aren't here to stay.
-Dad Brad

DAD JOKE 30

What did the ocean say to the beach?

Nothing, it just waved.

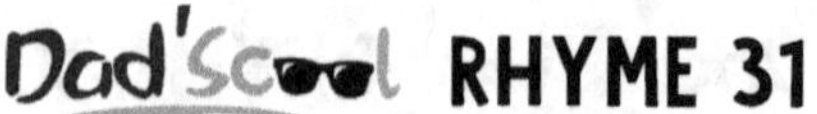

You'll spend a lot of time figuring out
Who you are and what you're about.
You'll adapt to others and be like your friends
But in the end...
Be who you feel you are and want to be.
That's the kind of life that's lived fully.
-Dad Brad

DAD JOKE 31

What does a cloud do when it gets an itch?

It finds the nearest skyscraper.

Never dim your light
So, others won't feel insecure.
You were born here on earth
To develop and share your worth.
Shine bright, it's your birthright.
-Dad Brad

DAD JOKE 32

What did Baby Corn say to Mama Corn?

Where's Pop Corn?

A lot of thought goes into the professional
We want to be. But in actuality,
More thought should go into WHO we want to be.
When we do this, the profession will come easily.
The money will flow freely and
You can give to others thankfully.
-Dad Brad

BE
WHO YOU
WANt to
BE

DAD JOKE 33

What do pre-teen ducks hate?

When their voice quacks.

Ideas not acted on are a dime a dozen.
What does a dime a dozen even mean?
It's something very common, of no great value.
Wait, an idea is of no value; is this true?
What about Apple, Tesla, and Amazon?
They were all an idea at first.
True, but without action an idea goes
To the graveyard, in a hurst.
The value comes when the idea goes into action.
Starting and doing is the best plan of action.
-Dad Brad

DAD JOKE 34

Where do you learn to make a banana split?

Sundae school.

Life will try and beat you down.
When it does, tell it to get out of town.
You'll get stronger battling what comes your way.
You might end up grateful for the struggle, one day.
It'll help you grow to who you're meant to be.
And remember, you'll always be loved by daddy.
-Dad Brad

Get outta TOWN!

DAD JOKE 35

Why couldn't the pony sing a lullaby?

She was a little horse.

Put the cap back on the toothpaste.
It's in bad taste, to get it all over the place.
Wipe it down out of the sink
And use the toilet brush after a stink.
-Dad Brad

DAD JOKE 36

What did one autumn leaf say to the other?

I'm falling for you.

How do you eat an elephant?
One bite at a time.
It's a phrase to help you realize
That no matter how giant the size,
The largeness of the task,
Step by step, bite by bite,
Is the best plan of attack.
You accomplish big things
By doing small things, consistently.
-Dad Brad

DAD JOKES 37

It was a terrible summer for Humpty Dumpty,
but he did have a great fall.

Keep your word, be one people can trust.
Do what you say, trust is a must.
Don't lose the trust others have in you.
It's hard to gain back, no matter the good you do.
You'll make mistakes as we all will.
Keeping your word is a valuable life skill.
-Dad Brad

DAD JOKE 38

Why do fathers take an extra pair of socks when they go golfing?

In case they get a hole in one.

Dad'scool RHYME 39

Gut feelings are like angels
Helping guide our way.
Follow them closely
And all will be okay.
-Dad Brad

DAD JOKE 39

Why was 6 afraid of 7?

Because 7,8,9.

 Dad'Scool RHYME 40

The love I have for you
Is something special and true.
Even though you think I'm a grumpy old man,
Know that I'm striving the best that I can,
To be the dad that we can both be proud of.
A good relationship is something to strive for,
There really isn't anything that I'd truly want more.
-Dad Brad

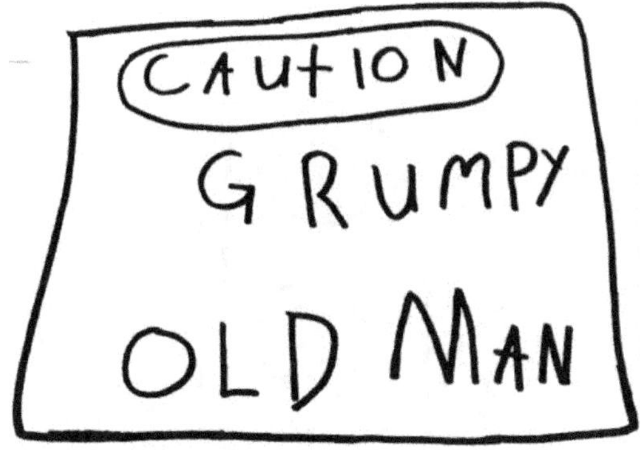

DAD JOKE 40

Why can't a leopard hide?

Because he's always spotted.

Life needs more greenlights.
Go for good grades.
Go for the lead in the play.
Go for the goal.
Go for the guy or girl.
Go for the homerun.
Find what sets fire to your heart,
Give it some gas and just start.
Go for it, you have the greenlight!
-Dad Brad

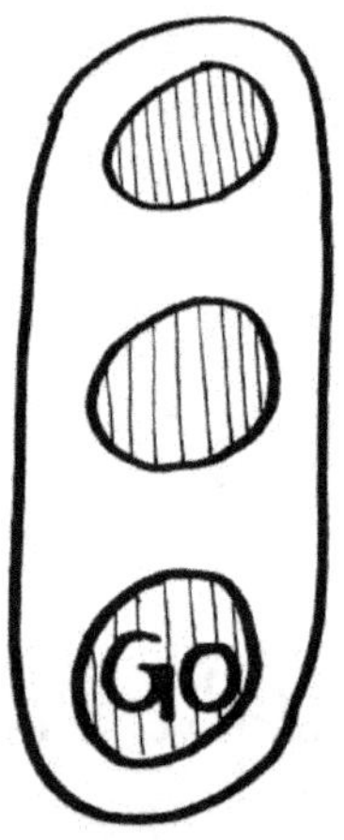

DAD JOKE 41

What do you call a cow eating grass?

A lawn moooo-er.

Lifting weights makes muscles weaker.
You're breaking them down.
It's the recovery phase when they turn around.
They rebuild and come back stronger.
It's the same for us.
Hard things shake us; they break us,
But they also make us.
-Dad Brad

DAD JOKE 42

*What did the earth scientist say when someone
asked what makes him happy?*

*"Well, I guess you could say the rotation
of earth really makes my day."*

It's Halloween time,
We get to dress up as who we want to be.
But honestly, in reality, that's every day, you see.
So put on your costume and be who you dream of being.
-Dad Brad

DAD JOKE 43

Why was the broom late to work?

It over swept.

RHYME 44

When birds fly,
They're high in the sky.
Do you ever wonder why?
Maybe they've mastered the thing,
Where they have the courage to spread their wings.
Be like the bird, overcome self-doubt,
Know what you're about.
Don't be scared to soar high above.
That natural feeling is one you'll love.
It's called being proud of who you are.
You're awesome and capable,
Now go fly to the stars.
-Dad Brad

DAD JOKE 44

Why did the scarecrow win an award?

Because he was outstanding in his field.

The leaves are falling; fall is in the air.
Trees are bare, lungs filled with cold air.
It's a great day to show others you care.
Find someone that is alone during the day.
Give them a compliment and say,
"Hey, can we be friends? Let's go play."
-Dad Brad

DAD JOKE 45

What did the evil chicken lay?

Deviled eggs.

Dad'scool RHYME 46

Starting out the day with a rhyme and a joke,
Helps our tired eyes be happy, they woke.
Be the reason someone smiles today.
At the end, your eyes will be tired and happy to close.
You'll feel accomplished of the days decisions you chose.
-Dad Brad

DAD JOKE 46

When does a joke become a dad joke?

When it becomes apparent.

Goblins and ghosts, pirates, and witches.
Halloween brings out the spooky, by definition.
Gobble up the good cause there's darkness in life,
But it helps us to better appreciate the light.
-Dad Brad

DAD JOKE 47

Why are pancakes good at baseball?

Because they have the best batter.

 RHYME 48

Listen quietly when others talk.
Be a friend that listens like a hawk.
Sometimes not having much to say
Is okay, because being a good listener,
Goes a long way.
-Dad Brad

DAD JOKE 48

Why do nurses like red crayons?

Because they have to draw blood.

 **RHYME 49**

Henry Ford once said;
"Whether you think you can or can't, you're right".
It's true. It's up to you, on what you do.
Believe in you because I do, too.
-Dad Brad

You're
Right...

DAD JOKE 49

What do you call a naughty lamb dressed
as a skeleton for Halloween?

Baaaaad to the bone.

Worry-wart.
Someone who worries about too many things
The monster under the bed, the thing someone said,
The bad test score in red.
Worry less, just give your best.
Focus on what you can change,
The rest is pointless and unneeded stress.
-Dad Brad

DAD JOKE 50

Why did the guy without his glasses fall down the well?

Because he didn't see that well.

There's magic in each moment
That's sometimes hard to see
Especially if you're always waiting
For the moments that are going to be.
Live in the present, that's why it's called a gift.
You're alive today, it's like you won the Genie's wish.
-Dad Brad

DAD JOKE 51

Why does Peter Pan get tired of flying?

Because he Neverlands.

We're always told to be kind to others.
To siblings, friends, to your dad and mother.
Yep, this is true,
But it also means to be kind to you!
-Dad Brad

DAD JOKE 52

Why did the bank teller lose his job on the first day?

Because an old lady asked him to check
her balance, so he pushed her over.

Today is a new beginning,
Let's start out winning.
Even if you feel like you've lost,
Realize you've won,
The moment the day has begun.
You're alive, you're here.
For that, be of good cheer.
-Dad Brad

DAD JOKE 53

What kind of music do chiropractors play at their office?

Hip Pop.

Dad'scool RHYME 54

Look for the good in people
Even though no one is perfect.
When you look for the good
The good you will get.
-Dad Brad

DAD JOKE 54

What kind of car does a rich sheep drive?

A Laaaaamborghini.

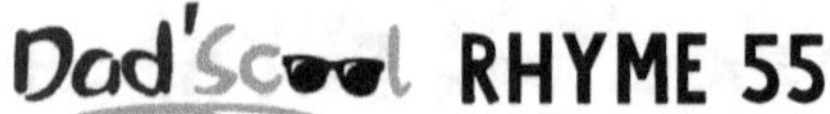

Dad'scool RHYME 55

Have good manners, it does matter.
There's a time and place to yell "hey, batter".
At a game you can scream and get rowdy,
Know your audience and act accordingly.
In class, be a little less loud; be polite,
Make us proud.
Give respect and respect you'll get.
-Dad Brad

DAD JOKE 55

What did one goldfish say to the
other goldfish in the tank?

Do you know how to drive this thing?

Read books.
They're a great escape for your mind.
Read ones that stretch your thinking.
Read ones that encourage imagination.
Read ones that teach you.
Read ones that motivate you.
Read ones that move you.
Read ones that entertain you.
Don't ever stop, reading, it's good to do
And is good for you.
-Dad Brad

DAD JOKE 56

My daughter said I just don't understand and that I should try walking in her shoes.

But I don't think they're going to fit.

When your parents seem strict
Here's the trick, don't get ticked,
With lessons they're trying to stick.
They have their own logic.
They're trying to get you to see
How to become the best you can be.
-Dad Brad

DAD JOKE 57

What do lions use to look at their manes?

MirRoars.

 RHYME 58

When it's time for decisions and a choice,
Pay attention to your inner voice.
It's the one connected spiritually,
It's in tune with your body, with you, mentally.
You'll often be right when you learn to recognize,
The subtle voice, the one that tries,
To guide you on the correct path
Or helps you back when you fall off the track.
Learn to listen to the voice inside.
It'll help you decide, it'll be your guide.
-Dad Brad

DAD JOKE 58

Why does a tall couple get along so well?

They can really see eye to eye.

Have a grateful heart.
It's the best way to start.
Be thankful for the good,
And learn from the bad.
Remember all the good you have.
-Dad Brad

DAD JOKE 59

Why couldn't a couple get married at the library?

It was all booked up.

Let's go! Let's go,
Let's be who we want to be.
Strive to be better than yesterday on 3.

1,2,3, Let's Go!
-Dad Brad

DAD JOKE 60

What vegetable is kind to everyone?

The sweet potato.

Dad'scool RHYME 61

Learn to love nature, go outside.
Pick up a ball, take your bike for a ride.
Go find bugs, pick rocks, and explore.
There's more to life than just being indoors.
There will always be time for work and chores,
Go take advantage of the beautiful outdoors.
-Dad Brad

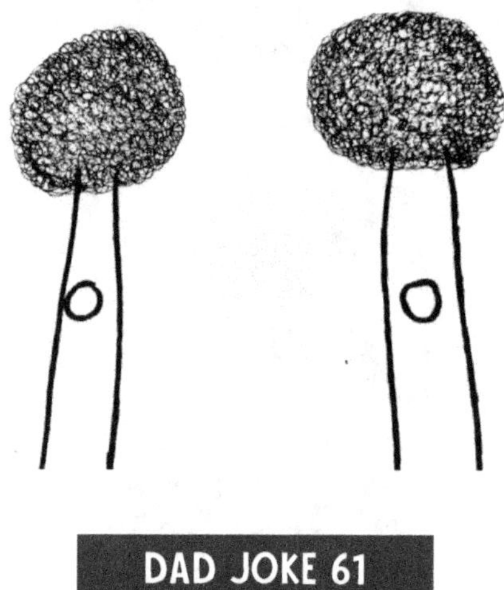

DAD JOKE 61

What did the dad say when someone complimented him on his hair cut?

"Thanks, but I cut them all."

Dad'scool RHYME 62

DAD JOKE 62

What is the best way to watch a fly-fishing tournament?

Live Stream.

Be a good loser.
You'll win even if you lose,
By having a good attitude.
Be a good person,
That is kind not rude.
-Dad Brad

DAD JOKE 63

Why do cows wear bells?

Because their horns don't work.

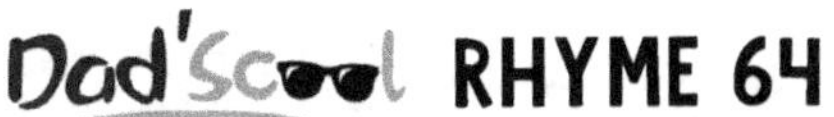

Be a good winner, you'll win more,
By showing, you're more
Than the number on the score board.
Be proud of your winning effort, for sure
Just don't be a winner, that's salty, and sore.
-Dad Brad

DAD JOKE 64

Did you hear the rumor about the butter?

Well, I'm not going to spread it.

Dad'scool RHYME 65

A Chameleon lizard molds and adapts.
It changes its hue, its brightness, the color on its back.
Be like the chameleon,
Adjust for different situations when changes come,
But always be you, don't change for anyone.
By being true to you,
You'll find the friends you're supposed to.
Not the ones that make you mold and adapt.
These kinds of friends can be a trap.
Be you and you'll find the ones that have your back.
-Dad Brad

DAD JOKE 65

My wife asked me to sync her phone.

She got mad when I threw it into the ocean.

Every day, go out of your way
To do something nice
Or have something nice to say.
Make someone's day today, and
Your own life will turn out better than okay.
-Dad Brad

DAD JOKE 66

What do you call someone with no body and no nose?

Nobody knows.

Love your life by living the life you love.
This is easiest by giving thanks above.
An attitude of gratitude is a great way to live.
Be grateful and thankfulness give.
-Dad Brad

DAD JOKE 67

I love dad jokes and puns.

They're how Eye Roll.

Dad'Scool RHYME 68

When you see dad mad,
Understand the pressure he has.
Sometimes adults get grumpy,
Because there's a lot going on.
They don't love you any less,
You'll always share a special bond.
Hopefully the grumpiness won't last too long.
-Dad Brad

DAD JOKE 68

My dad was just reminiscing about the herb garden his parents had while growing up.

Good thymes.

Dad'**Scool** RHYME 69

Don't stress the small stuff. Most stuff is small.
Even the big stuff in 5 years, won't matter much at all.
Life goes on so control what you can.
The other stuff is out of your control; stick to your plan.
-Dad Brad

DAD JOKE 69

While barbequing hamburgers, my dad told
everyone not to forget the pickle.

He said it's kind of a big dill.

 RHYME 70

Life is fun, bask in the sun.
The day will come,
When life kicks your bum.
It happens to everyone.
A positive attitude,
Helps bring back the bright sun.
-Dad Brad

DAD JOKE 70

What do you call a lazy kangaroo?

A pouch potato.

Be happy today,
It's a new day.
The old one is gone,
cherish the good and
Toss the bad away.
-Dad Brad

DAD JOKE 71

Did you hear about the cat who ate a ball of yarn?

She ended up having mittens.

Dad'scool RHYME 72

Listen to your teacher and show respect.
Raise your hand every chance you get.
Pay attention to what they teach.
Do good in school and in the summer,
You've earned time at the beach.
-Dad Brad

DAD JOKE 72

How do you tell the difference between
an alligator and a crocodile?

One you see later and one you see after a while.

Life is good, keep this attitude,
Yes, there are days that are just rude.
There will always be good and always be bad
But you'll feel more fulfilled when you think life is rad.
-Dad Brad

DAD JOKE 73

Why can't you trust an atom?

Because they make up everything.

Opportunity knocks, have a welcoming door.
It's gives chances to those who have prepared more.
Yes, you can get lucky,
But when luck meets preparation,
That's the best opportunity.
-Dad Brad

DAD JOKE 74

I used to hate facial hair.

But then it grew on me.

Dad'scool RHYME 75

Dad has a wish for you.
He wants your life to be how you want it to.
He wants your dreams big; He wants your worries small.
He wants you to know, daddy loves you, most of all.
P.S.
This rhyme is inspired by
A favorite song,
To where we all sing along.
'My Wish' by Rascal Flatts.
And in that, you'll find,
Many wishes I want to come true, for you.
-Dad Brad

DAD JOKE 75

What did the duck say when she bought lipstick?

Put it on my bill.

RHYME 76

Happiness=The State of Being Happy.
Not an award you get when you reach a milestone,
A goal or accomplishment.
It's deciding every day that happiness you'll get.
Sure, you'll feel good when you reach a certain point.
But it'll wear off and life will disappoint.
You'll start all over and search for it again,
Real happiness is being happy with
What you are and what you have within.
-Dad Brad

DAD JOKE 76

Why are spiders so smart?

They can find all the answers on the web.

Never watch the last strike go by.
If you go down swinging,
Hang your head up high.
Life is the same. It's like a game.
You win some, you lose some and
You'll feel the strike out shame.
Then, the moment comes
Where you knock it out of the park.
Run those bases proudly and shine your light in the dark.
Cherish good moments, learn from the rest.
You'll spend each day knowing, you gave your best.
-Dad Brad

DAD JOKE 77

What did the cow use during its math test?

A cow-culator.

Take a stand,
Stand for what you believe.
When you don't stand for something,
You can fall for anything.
Stand for what you want to be and want to achieve.
-Dad Brad

DAD JOKE 78

Why do seagulls fly over the sea?

Because if they flew over the bay, they'd be called bagels.

We Wish You a Merry Christmas
Is a song we sing and cheer.
Joyfully and triumphantly for all to hear.
Let's keep the cheerfulness going
Throughout the whole year.
-Dad Brad

DAD JOKE 79

I'm reading a book about anti-gravity.

It's impossible to put down.

 RHYME 80

Stand up when meeting someone new.
Look them in the eye, it's the polite thing to do.
Respect is earned where respect is given.
That's a respectful life, worth living.
-Dad Brad

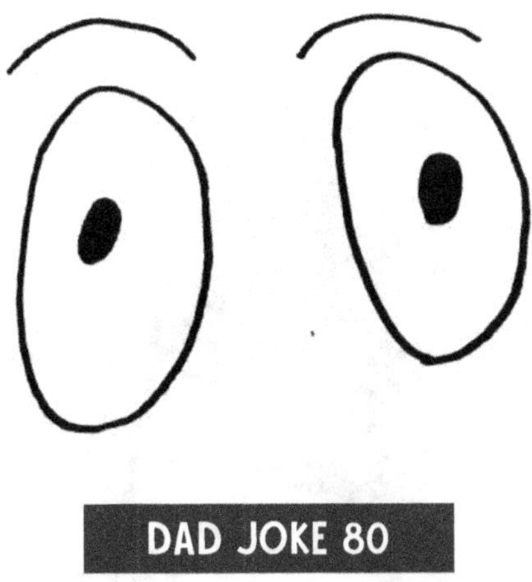

DAD JOKE 80

Which is faster, hot or cold?

Hot, because you can catch a cold.

Dad'scool RHYME 81

Give forgiveness,
Just as you want to be forgiven.
Judging others for how they're living,
Isn't how to spend the time you've been given.
Try your best, they most likely are, too.
Give forgiveness, just as you want it given to you.
-Dad Brad

DAD JOKE 81

How do you organize a space party?

You plan it.

Do hard things.
They make you better.
Avoid the easy road and
You'll better whether the weather.
The storms of life will come,
By doing hard things
You'll recognize the rising of the sun.
-Dad Brad

DAD JOKE 82

What do clouds do when they become rich?

They make it rain.

Toddlers ask "why" about everything.
It's cute and can be annoying.
In truth, they're just trying to learn and figure out life.
Be like a toddler, be curious, keep asking "why."
-Dad Brad

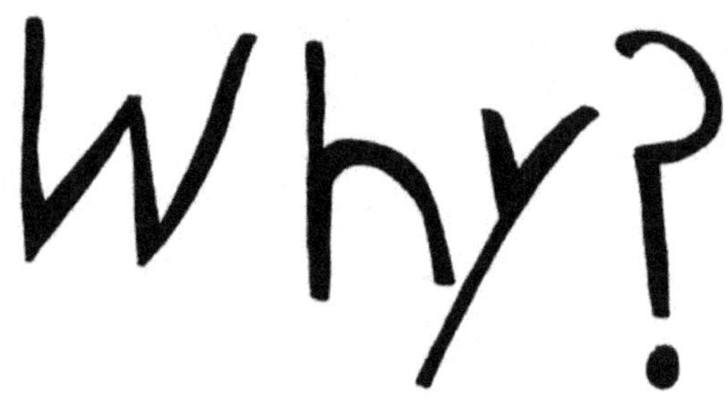

DAD JOKE 83

What does a baby computer call his father?

Data.

White snow, bright lights,
Leaving out cookies for Santa to bite.
There's so much magic to the night.
Remember the true reason for the season.
It's about a gift and giving.
It's about life and eternal living.
It's about believing.
What a sight, to see the magic of the night.
-Dad Brad

DAD JOKE 84

What did the zero say to the eight?

Nice belt.

Dad'Scool RHYME 85

Be goofy and funny and fun to be around.
Everyone laughs at a silly class clown
But do so respectfully,
Lift others up, don't knock them down.
-Dad Brad

DAD JOKE 85

What time did the man go to the dentist?

Tooth-Hurty.

Pick up your head and keep going.
Even on the days when it's most boring.
When life gets hard, go step by step, look ahead.
You'll get through it, an old, wise dad, said.
-Dad Brad

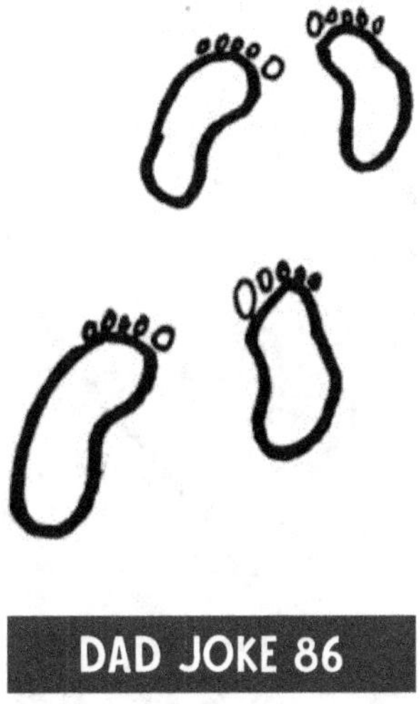

DAD JOKE 86

What did the fisherman say to the magician?

Pick a cod, any cod.

Dad'Scool RHYME 87

Real success is found in different things.
But honestly, it's not found in actual things.
Things are nice and fun to have,
But in the end, if you had peace, health, and love,
Then you experienced true happiness from above.
-Dad Brad

DAD JOKE 87

Why was the laptop late to school?

It had a hard drive.

Life is more than what's behind you.
It's more than what's directly in front of you, too.
There is much more to life than
What you're feeling at this moment.
Because this moment is just a moment.
Enjoy, learn, and move on from it.
Feels good, don't it?
Mmmm, hey, let's be late to school
And go get a donut.
-Dad Brad

DAD JOKE 88

What did the big flower say to the small flower?

Hey there, bud.

Dad'Scool RHYME 89

Be like the ocean who doesn't care who you are
It waves to others from near or far.
It doesn't change when others try and persuade it to,
It consistently just keeps waving at you.
-Dad Brad

DAD JOKE 89

Why does everyone like being around the volcano?

Because it's so lava-able.

Dad'scool RHYME 90

Our minds are simple and hold one thought at a time.
Make it a good one, full of positive rhymes.
When the negative creeps in, as it surely will,
You'll be happy you've developed a happy mindset skill.
Sometimes easier said than done.
Sometimes the negative weighs a ton.
If it gets too heavy, please talk with someone,
But overall, life is meant for positive fun.
-Dad Brad

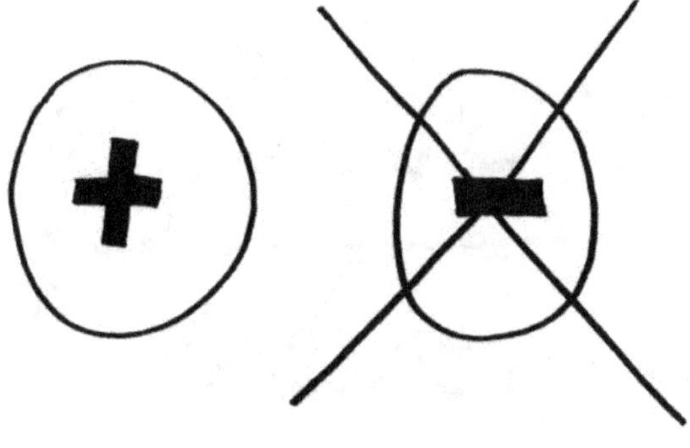

DAD JOKE 90

Why was the snail cut from the race team?

It was too sluggish.

Sibling's fight, sometimes a lot
Is it built into their DNA or self-taught?
As time passes, hopefully great friends, you'll be.
Try now to treat each other kindly, pretty, please.
-Dad Brad

DAD JOKE 91

Why don't crabs give to charity?

Because they're shellfish.

Do it right the first time.
Don't do something halfway and expect a big payday.
If it's worth doing at all, it's your call, to give 100% effort,
Your best overall.
-Dad Brad

DAD JOKE 92

What do sprinters eat before a big race?

Nothing, they fast.

Dad'Scool RHYME 93

Boring is entering the pool from the stairs.
Take a leap, jump up, and get some big air.
Yell "cannon ball" and make a splash, everywhere.
You're a kid at the pool without a care.
Live your life the same, that's my prayer.
-Dad Brad

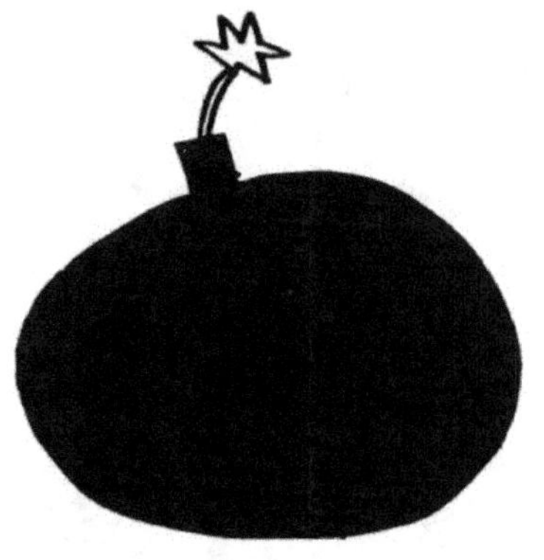

DAD JOKE 93

Want to hear a joke about a pizza?

Never mind, it's too cheesy.

Words matter.
Hurtful words splatter.
Kind words flatter.
Use words that lift up
Not words that drag down.
Be someone that others want to be around.
-Dad Brad

DAD JOKE 94

Have you heard of the lady who only eats plants?

You've probably never heard of herbivore?

Give grace, gracefully.
Give it to yourself, to others, and to me.
We all need grace every day.
Try to go out of your way
In your actions and in what you say
To show kindness and compassion.
It'll bring you a lot of satisfaction.
-Dad Brad

DAD JOKE 95

What do you call a magic dog?

A labracadabrador.

Dad'Scool RHYME 96

The constant of life is that it will always change.
Being able to roll with it, is the name of the game.
Papa always said "tough times don't last
But tough people do."
It's true.
When times get rough, hang on.
It'll get better for you.
-Dad Brad

DAD JOKE 96

Why is a fish easy to weigh?

Because it has its own scales.

You attract what you give
So, give what you want.
Being a giver is a good way to live.
That includes you giving yourself
The same kind of love.
Super-duper love like when
A cold hand fits into a warm glove.
-Dad Brad

DAD JOKE 97

The other day I was out washing the car with my son.

He said, "Dad, can't you just use a sponge."

Dad'Scool RHYME 98

When one door closes, keep your eyes open.
Look for another door that's in motion.
If it's broken, maybe a window is the token,
To a new opportunity, that'll be awoken.
-Dad Brad

DAD JOKE 98

My mon took me to the doctor for a bladder infection.

The doc said, "urine trouble."

Dad'scool RHYME 99

Self-doubt. Delete it.
You don't need it.
Tell it to beat it.
Get out of town.
It's not wanted around.
Turn the frown upside down.
You're a king, a queen,
Put on the crown.
-Dad Brad

DAD JOKE 99

What do you call your dad when he falls through the ice?

A Popsicle.

I'm so thankful for you, for what you do,
For who are, for driving with me in this car.
For being a shining star, for sharing dad jokes
And motivating quotes.
Taking you to school is a highlight of my day
I love ya, shine bright, today.
-Dad Brad

DAD JOKE 100

Why did the football coach go to the bank?

To get his quarterback.

Dad'<u>Scool</u> RHYME 101

DAD JOKE 101

Air for your car tires at the gas station used to be free.

Now it cost $2 because of inflation.

It's cold, winter is here. Gloomy and dreary is near.
Change your mindset and think of beautiful white snow.
If that doesn't work, forget it, off to the beach we go.
Just kidding. Time for school.
Toes in the sand does sound fun, though.
-Dad Brad

DAD JOKE 102

Why did the orange lose the race?

It ran out of juice.

Dad'scool RHYME 103

Know that you're loved
From many here, and many up above.
You have angels cheering you on
And people here, full of love.
It might be a parent, a sibling, or
A friend. A teacher, another student,
A grandparent, or your twin.
Just know you're cared about.
Always and forever.
You are loved, without a doubt.
-Dad Brad

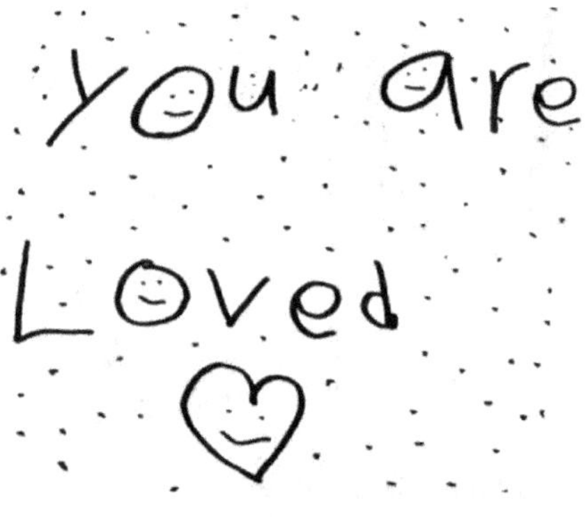

DAD JOKE 103

How do you fix a pumpkin with a hole in it?

With a pumpkin patch.

Make friends with many, be a friend to all.
Most importantly, even the #1 call,
Is to be friends with you, look in the mirror, stand tall.
-Dad Brad

DAD JOKE 104

Where do boats go when they get hurt?

To the dock.

Keep your promises
To yourself and to others
Keep them to your friends
And especially, your mothers.
-Dad Brad

DAD JOKE 105

I'm so good at sleeping, I can do it with my eyes closed.

Dad'Scool RHYME 106

You'll make mistakes, all of us do.
It's how you handle them that defines you.
Learn, and move on; that's the best thing to do.
Your mistakes are lessons; they don't define you.
-Dad Brad

DAD JOKE 106

What has ears but can't hear?

A cornfield.

When life gives you lemons, make lemonade.
When life gives you, an apple, make Snapple.
When life gives you grapes, put them in your crepe.
When life gives you a mango, go dance the Tango.
When life gives you a banana, take a vacation in a cabana
When life gives you a cantaloupe, tell a dad joke.
Life will come fast at every angle.
Sometimes it's messy and you'll get all tangled.
Look to the bright side; there is always one,
Cause focusing on the negative is boring and dumb.
-Dad Brad

DAD JOKE 107

What state is known for its small drinks?

Minnesota.

 Dad'Scool RHYME 108

Visualize is how you realize
The daunting dreams when you
Close your eyes that are high in the sky.
See them in your mind before you try.
Others will wonder why
You're one who isn't afraid to try?
It's because you've already seen
The winning results in your mind.
-Dad Brad

DAD JOKE 108

What did the house wear to its own house party?

Address.

Dad'Scool RHYME 109

How do you spell success?
S-U-C...No. It starts with H and ends with S
It's pronounced H-A-P-P-I-N-E-S-S.
The dictionary might spell it differently
But *H-A-P-P-I-N-E-S-S*
Is the true definition of success.
-Dad Brad

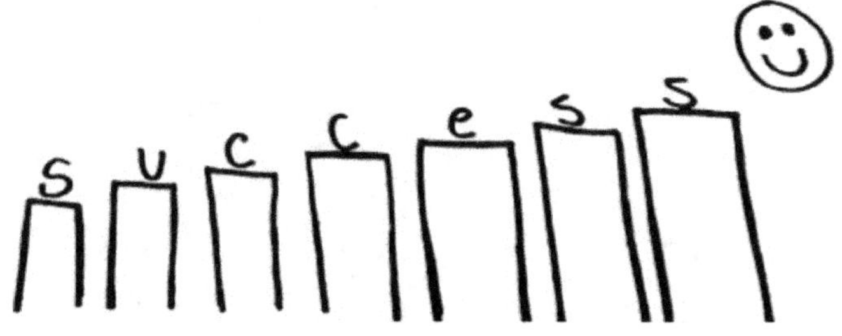

DAD JOKE 109

What do you say to a rabbit on its birthday?

Hoppy Birthday.

The world is lucky to have you.
You'll move mountains in all you do.
You're also lucky to have another day
Keep this mindset in all you do and say,
And cherish each moment every day.
-Dad Brad

DAD JOKE 110

What type of tree can you fit in your hand?

A palm tree.

Dad'scool RHYME 111

When introduced to someone new
Remember their name, have it stick like glue.
Oh, and when calling them by their name,
Look them in the eye, too.
-Dad Brad

DAD JOKE 111

Which state do you think has the most streets?

Rhode Island.

It's great to create.
Create love, not hate.
Create bridges, not gates.
Try to relate to friends and your mate.
Use your imagination every day.
Create a life you never want to escape.
-Dad Brad

DAD JOKE 112

How do you make the seven even?

You take away the s.

Dad'scool RHYME 113

Be happy, be sad
Be hopeful, be mad.
Be energetic, be lazy
Be joyful, be crazy.
Be outgoing, be shy
Be the funny gal or guy.
Feel it all, be it all,
Be you, in all you do.
-Dad Brad

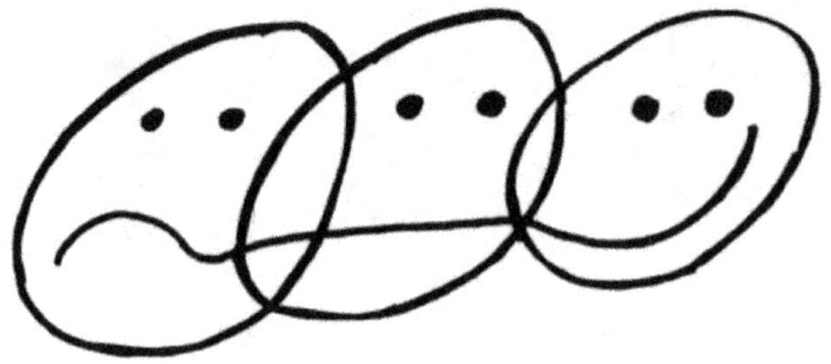

DAD JOKE 113

Where do math teachers like to vacation?

Times Square.

 Dad'Scool RHYME 114

A thank you will go a long way
It's the proper thing to say,
After someone went out of their way
To improve your day.
-Dad Brad

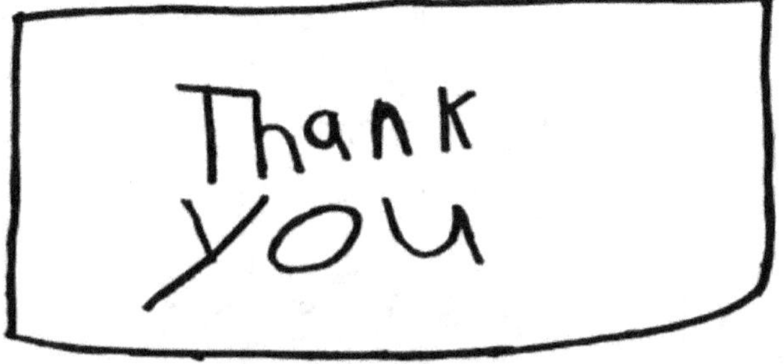

DAD JOKE 114

What kind of car delivers eggs?

Yolkswagon.

Dad'Scool RHYME 115

Take off your shoes when you enter the house,
In case you stepped in dog doo when out and about.
Just as stinky shoes bring a bad doubt,
so does talking about others when they're not around.
Don't gossip or treat others rude,
Especially when they're not in the same room.
If they're not around to defend themselves
Don't talk about them or anyone else.
-Dad Brad

DAD JOKE 115

Why did the bicycle fall over?

It was two tired.

External validation, what does it mean?
It's worrying about being accepted by others,
Which isn't a good thing.
Be friendly, have friends, but don't mold to fit in.
Be who you are and be happy within.
-Dad Brad

DAD JOKE 116

Why was the rabbit late for her date?

She was having a bad hare day.

Dad'Scool RHYME 117

If the truth hurts,
It still needs to be said.
You'll feel bad keeping it in your head,
It'll make you frustrated.
Get it out and move on ahead.
You'll feel better by getting it out,
Be truthful in all you're about.
-Dad Brad

DAD JOKE 117

Why did the shark say his lunch tasted funny?

Because he ate a clownfish.

Dad'scool RHYME 118

Drink lots of water.
Some days more when the weather is hotter.
Some days you won't bother.
An apple a day, keeps the doctor away
But drinking enough water each day,
Keeps you hydrated and healthy to go and play.
-Dad Brad

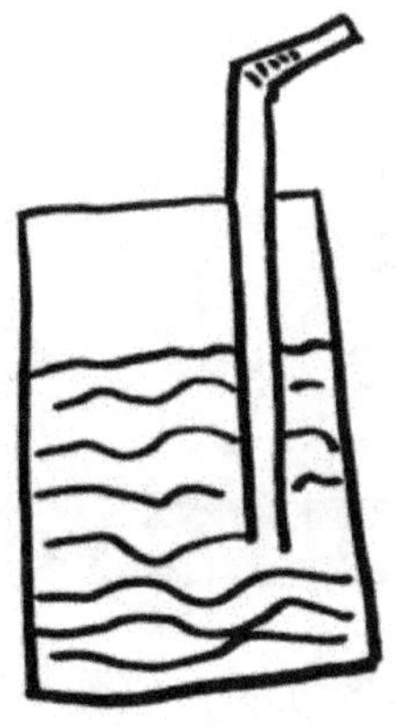

DAD JOKE 118

Why are bees' hair so sticky?

Because they use honeycombs.

Dad'scool RHYME 119

I want to teach you
A new way to spell Impossible.
Put a space in-between the M and the P.
You'll see the word as a new possibility.
Instead of impossible, you'll read,
I'm-Possible. Now go believe.
-Dad Brad

I'm Possible

DAD JOKE 119

Patient: Will I be able to play the piano after the operation?

Doctor: Yes, of course.

Patient: That's awesome, because I couldn't before.

Dad'Scool RHYME 120

You've heard the term fearless,
The trick is actually to fear, less.
There will always be things that scare us
But learning to do, despite the fear,
Is a key to success and happiness.
-Dad Brad

DAD JOKE 120

Do you know what the leading cause of dry skin is?

A towel.

Dads get mad.
It's like a built in pre-fab, when he becomes a dad.
At times, you'll think of him as an ornery old man,
Truth is, he's trying the best he can,
To help you grow into your best version.
Give him some grace, and he'll give it, too.
He wants the best for you; he's trying the best he can do.
-Dad Brad

DAD JOKE 121

What kind of shoes do burglars wear?

Sneakers.

Go at God's speed.
He and your mother know what you truly need.
Don't be afraid to get on your knees
To ask for help, give thanks and plead.
God knows best, and so does your mommy.
-Dad Brad

DAD JOKE 122

What do you call a pig in karate class?

Pork Chops.

Dad'Scool RHYME 123

Sometimes you'll have to say no, to say yes.
Sacrifice other things for what you want best.
It's okay if you turn down something good,
For something that could be,
It might turn out to be a greater opportunity.
-Dad Brad

DAD JOKE 123

Son: I'm hungry.

Dad: Hi hungry, I'm Dad. Nice to meet you.

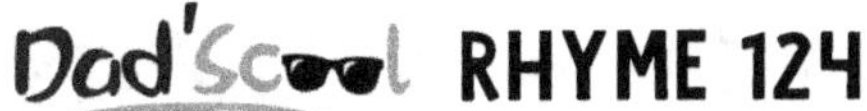

Dad'scool RHYME 124

Love is powerful.
Use it wisely, give it often.
Love is life's magic potion.
-Dad Brad

DAD JOKE 124

How do trees get online to check their Tree-mail?

They just log on.

Dad'scool RHYME 125

You become like those you hang around.
Want to be in a circus? Be friends with a clown.
You become the sum of those you're with most
Pick good friends who push you to improve,
Rather than stay still and coast.
Be someone others want to be with,
Help them be better, help them develop their gifts.
-Dad Brad

DAD JOKE 125

The numbers 19 and 20 got into a fight.

21.

Life moves fast and can make you dizzy.
Don't spend it always being too busy.
Take some time in the morning or evening
To smell the flowers or see something pretty.
Enjoy the small moments, breathe in, enjoy living.
-Dad Brad

DAD JOKE 126

Mountains aren't funny.

They're hill areas.

Dad'Scool RHYME 127

Open the door for people behind.
Even when in a hurry, it's better to be kind.
Simple things make all the difference,
Even when it's an inconvenience.
You'll feel better throughout the day
And maybe inspire another
To pay it forward, along their way.
-Dad Brad

DAD JOKE 127

What are slippers made from?

Banana peels.

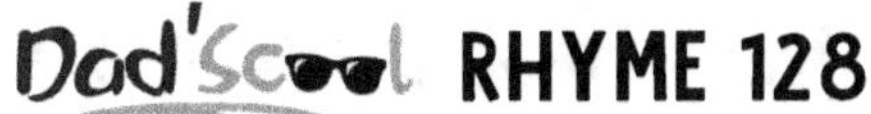

Dad'Scool RHYME 128

Yoga stretches your body,
Learning stretches your mind.
Sitting around, being lazy gets you behind,
To the last of the line.
Taking a break is good and fine
But challenging, stretching, and striving,
Makes you feel alive.
Have the drive to realize,
You're capable of all you can visualize.
-Dad Brad

DAD JOKE 128

What did the police officer say to his belly button?

You're under a vest.

Dad'Scool RHYME 129

It's a fine line to be
Confident and humble at the same time.
Don't be cocky but do know you are prime.
You're special, as is everyone, in their own way.
Know your worth, each and every day.
-Dad Brad

DAD JOKE 129

Knock, knock

Who's there?

Figs.

Figs, who?

Figs the doorbell, it's broken.

You can accomplish anything.
Trust your heart, put your mind to it.
Work hard and help others do it.
-Dad Brad

DAD JOKE 130

Why is the barber always first to work?

He knows a shortcut.

It takes the same amount of work
To be happy or mad.
Put the effort into being glad
For all the blessings you have
It'll change your outlook,
You'll be more joyful than sad.
-Dad Brad

DAD JOKE 131

My dad tripped and fell so I asked him if he was alright?

He said, "No. I'm half left."

You're great, remember this.
Give yourself and hug and a kiss.
Don't look for others approval,
You'll always be searching, it's brutal.
You're truly one of kind, a rare jewel.
-Dad Brad

DAD JOKE 132

What do you call a cow in a tornado?

A milkshake.

Dad'Scool RHYME 133

Of all the prized things there are,
Room full of toys, a new bike, a fast car.
There is one that is more valuable, by far.
It's not something that you can buy,
Rather it's something known to fly.
Once it's gone you can't get it back.
Life gets busy and it's something you'll lack.
We all have the same amount in a day
So, use it wisely, Okay.
I'll give you a clue, a rhyme.
The most cherished thing isn't a thing,
It's TIME.
-Dad Brad

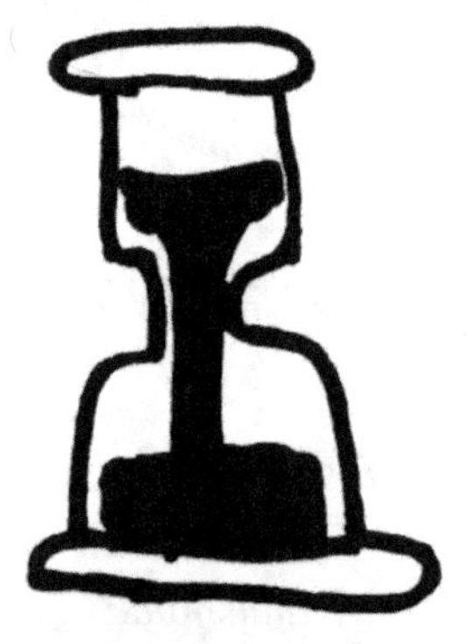

DAD JOKE 133

How do angels greet each other?

Halo.

Pay yourself first when you get paid.
Start early to get financial freedom made.
-Dad Brad

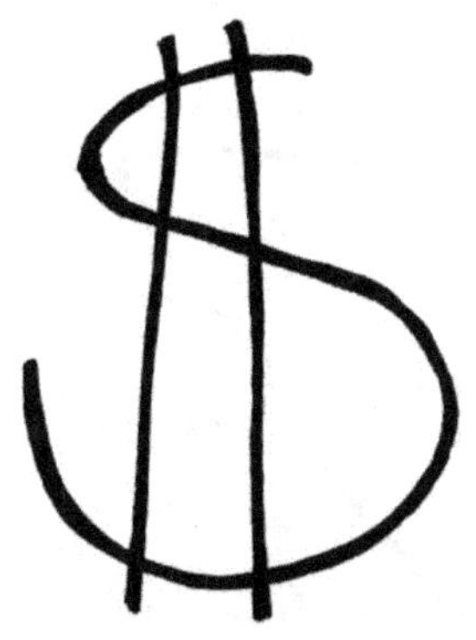

DAD JOKE 134

Knock, Knock.

Who's there?

Ice cream.

Ice cream who?

Ice cream if you don't let me in.

Let go of grudges; they're a waste of time.
Instead, use that time to run, skip and climb.
Good friends are worth gold so don't spend a dime,
On others who belittle, they're not worth your time.
-Dad Brad

DAD JOKE 135

The other day I accidentally handed my wife
a glue stick instead of her lipstick.

She still isn't talking to me.

Life is passing by.
Don't get your head stuck in clouds up in the sky.
Look to the future as a positive,
But live in the now, that's your life to live.
-Dad Brad

DAD JOKE 136

What do you call a spaghetti look alike?

An impasta.

Dad'Scool RHYME 137

Say please.
Say thank you.
Say excuse me.
Say I'm happy to.
Offer condolences.
Ask for help and offer help.
Say yes to good.
Learn to say no when you should.
-Dad Brad

Please
and
Thank you !

DAD JOKE 137

How do you put an alien baby back to sleep?

You rocket.

Be better than yesterday, that's the goal to shoot for.
Each day, strive to improve a little more.
Not every moment you need to keep score,
But remember yesterday and today be more.
-Dad Brad

Be
better
than Yesterday

DAD JOKE 138

How did the rabbit get across the ocean?

By hareplane.

*Your sense of humor
Is to amuse, not abuse.
Be nice with your jokes.
Avoid ones that poke.
Use your humor so others
Laugh and you'll laugh, too.
That's what great comedians do.
-Dad Brad*

DAD JOKE 139

I tried to take a picture of the fog.

I mist.

RHYME 140

Turn off the tap when brushing your teeth.
Don't keep the water running when washing them clean.
Water is precious, a valuable thing.
We're fortunate to have it so accessible.
Without it, we'd be in big trouble.
-Dad Brad

DAD JOKE 140

Why don't ants ever get sick?

Because they have anty-bodies.

Dad'scool RHYME 141

Happiness comes from you
Not in what others do or don't do.
Fill your life with things you enjoy.
Treat life as one giant, favorite toy.
-Dad Brad

DAD JOKE 141

In England they call it a lift. In the United
States it's called an elevator.

I guess they're just raised differently.

 RHYME 142

Powerful Beyond Measure
That is what you are.
You're as powerful as you believe
and will go extremely far.
Have confidence and know your worth.
You were born a miracle birth.
Shine your light, don't ever dim it down,
So, others won't feel insecure,
The brighter you shine; the world becomes brighter.
-Dad Brad

DAD JOKE 142

What did the nut say when chasing the other nut?

I'm a cashew.

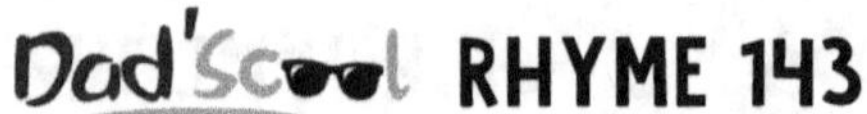

RHYME 143

There's a circle that becomes our home,
It's called our comfort zone.
Big Dan taught me when I was younger,
Taking a step out of it, will do wonders.
Sure, it's easier living safe and comfy
But, learning to live in discomfort
Gets us where we want to be.
-Dad Brad

DAD JOKE 143

What do you call a baby potato?

A tator tot.

Enjoy.
Go about your day, "in, joy."
Enjoy life.
-Dad Brad

DAD JOKE 144

What did the drummer name his twin daughters?

Anna 1, Anna 2.

Dad'Scool RHYME 145

Don't be afraid of change,
Cause each day is hardly the same.
Adapting to new elements
Is the name of the game.
To stay the same would be strange.
Learn, grow, adapt, and change.
-Dad Brad

DAD JOKE 145

Does anyone need an ark?

If so, I Noah guy.

Others might seem to be in charge,
Your parents, your teachers, coaches, and bosses.
But it's important to realize, who the real boss is.
It's you, no one else but you.
You decide what kind of person you develop into.
You decide what you get out of life
You decide your happiness, despite the struggles,
And the things that don't go right.
You decide how to lay your head down at night.
Be happy with the person you are and will become.
Knowing you're in charge is exciting and fun.
You're the real boss, the decision maker, #1
-Dad Brad

DAD JOKE 146

What lights up a soccer stadium?

A soccer match.

Have pride in all you say and do.
Have pride in your appearance, too.
Doesn't mean you have to become obsessed
With wearing the best or being better than the rest
But care for yourself, so you feel impressed.
-Dad Brad

DAD JOKE 147

Does the dairy farmer like corny jokes?

No, he prefers them to be cheesy.

The true kind of charity
Is where you're kind
Because you want to be.
A cheerful giver is the best kind.
It's good for your heart,
Great for your mind.
True charity is to be kind.
-Dad Brad

DAD JOKE 148

What do you call a bull taking a nap?

A Bull-Dozer.

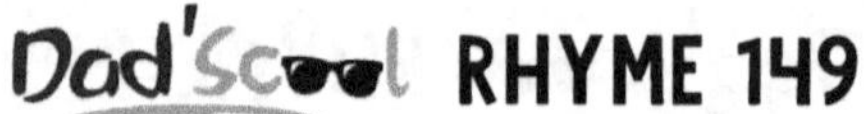 Dad's cool RHYME 149

It's never too late to start again.
Some plans don't work out,
They break, they bend.
That's okay because you'll learn from them.
Dust off your shoes and start again, my friend.
-Dad Brad

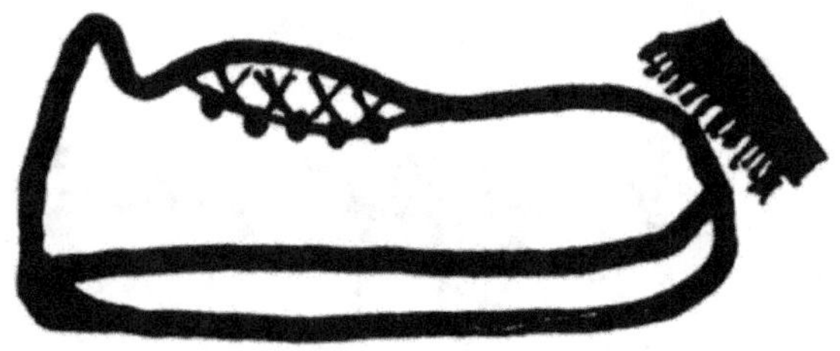

DAD JOKE 149

Did you hear about the restaurant on the moon?

Great food, no atmosphere.

Fail.
Yes, you heard that right,
Failing isn't bad if you've given
An honest effort, gave all you had.
You didn't fail, you learned.
Eventually, success will take a turn.
-Dad Brad

FAil = Learn

DAD JOKE 150

What's orange and sounds like a parrot?

A carrot.

Dad'Scool RHYME 151

If you don't know, it's okay to say it.
You don't need to act like you know it.
When you make a mistake,
It's okay to admit you made it.
You don't need to feel like
You're the only one mistaken.
-Dad Brad

DAD JOKE 151

*A Mexican magician said he'll disappear
on the count of three.*

*Uno, Dos...Poof.
He disappeared without a tres.*

Love you.
I love you and want you to love you, too.
-Dad Brad

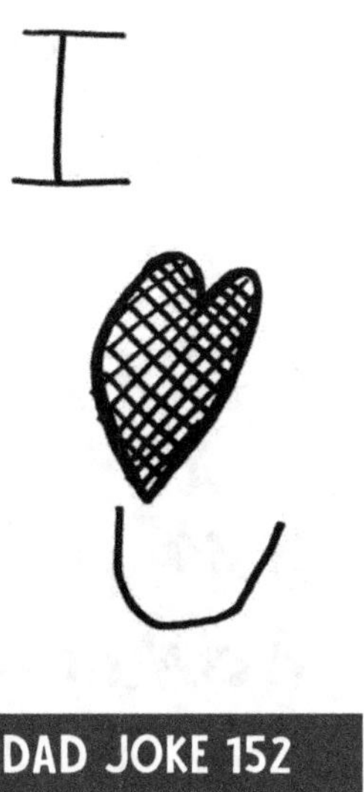

DAD JOKE 152

I'm trying to organize a hide-and-seek tournament.

Good players are really hard to find.

This is your life, so live it.
Each new morning,
Give thanks for the time given.
Appreciate life by fully livin'.
Savor the sweet moments
As you do your favorite doughnut.
-Dad Brad

DAD JOKE 153

What does a baker like to get on Valentine's Day?

Flour.

Open your heart,
Experience the greatness of life.
You might get some wounds,
Some cuts, from a sharp knife.
But there's so much good
That you'll want to feel and see
An open heart makes this a possibility.
-Dad Brad

DAD JOKE 154

What do you call a magician who loses his magic?

Ian.

Dad'Scool RHYME 155

Sometimes life isn't what you expect it to be.
It doesn't go as planned; it can make you ornery.
The trick is, honestly,
To look at the good, go on with your life joyfully.
This can be easier said than done,
So, start by doing more stuff that's fun.
-Dad Brad

DAD JOKE 155

I went on date last night with a girl from the Zoo.

It was great, she's a keeper.

The world is lucky to have you.
You'll move mountains in all you do.
You're also lucky to have another day
Keep this mindset in what you do and say,
And value the moments of each day.
-Dad Brad

DAD JOKE 156

I was wondering why my frisbee kept
looking bigger and bigger?

And then it hit me.

Dad'scool RHYME 157

As a kid, Nana would tell me,
You're either moving forward or backwards,
Being stagnant, isn't a possibility.
You'll take two steps ahead and maybe one step behind.
But keep moving, keep striving, stay with the grind.
One step after the other is best.
We're here to enjoy, to improve and to make progress.
-Dad Brad

Step 1

Step 2
Step 3
Step 4
step 5

DAD JOKE 157

I was at the park yesterday with my dog and
the ducks kept trying to bite him.

I guess that's what I get for buying a pure bread dog.

Haters gonna hate
That's what they do.
They're jealous of others, and you, too.
They see the good you're about
They throw fits, scream, and shout.
Haters gonna hate, that's what they do.
Never let them stop you from being you.
-Dad Brad

See Ya Later, Haters

DAD JOKE 158

What kind of farm animal keeps the best time?

A watch dog.

Develop your talents.
You've been given many gifts.
Share them with the world.
Practice and persist.
They get better the more you use them,
Share your talents again and again.
-Dad Brad

DAD JOKE 159

What's worse than finding a worm in your apple?

Finding half a worm in your apple.

 RHYME 160

Often problems come in disguise.
It might just be an opportunity before your eyes.
Work through the problem and open the door,
To new possibilities and more.
-Dad Brad

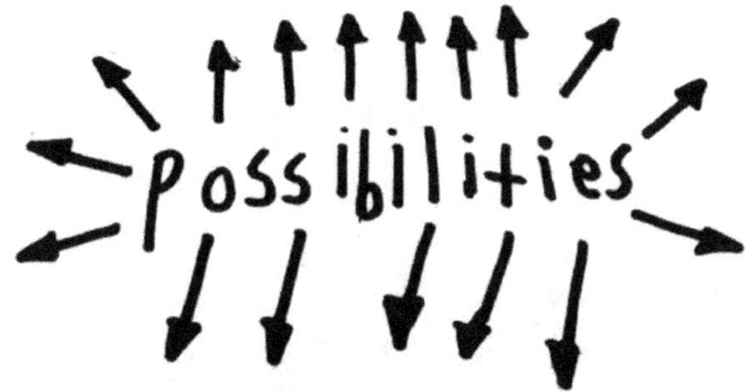

DAD JOKE 160

*What is the difference between a poorly dressed man
on a tricycle and a nicely dresses man on a bicycle?*

Attire.

Dad'scool RHYME 161

Life is tough and sometimes not fun,
But tomorrow isn't far off, and the morning will come.
There is something renewing with the rising of the sun.
Day by day is how it's done.
-Dad Brad

Life
is
tough
but
So are
You !

DAD JOKE 161

Why did the family picture go to jail?

Because it was framed.

Mothers were put here on earth
As the absolute best thing to give birth.
They're special, they're kind; they're one of a kind.
In my mind, they're the best of humankind.
Are they perfect? No, no one is.
But stay close to your mom,
Cause they're as close as it gets.
-Dad Brad

DAD JOKE 162

Where do rabbits go after the get married?

On a bunny-moon.

Dad'scool RHYME 163

Lead with appreciation for the new day.
An attitude of gratitude is the best way.
Start on your knees and pray
Give thanks for another day.
-Dad Brad

Thanks
For
Today

DAD JOKE 163

I feel good about what I did today. I gave away all my old batteries.

Free of charge.

Love is a verb, it's an action word.
Words are easy to say.
Actions mean more than words.
If you want love to be a thing,
It needs to be an action you do,
Action trumps words and ideas, too.
-Dad Brad

DAD JOKE 164

What do you call an American Bee?

A USB.

If A=1, and B=2, then C=3. When you add a
Number to each letter in the alphabet and
Take the word attitude, what do you get?
It equals 100 or 100%.
Which means regardless of talent
Attitude will be triumphant.
-Dad Brad

DAD JOKE 165

What did the stand-up comedian say
when he got to the hospital?

I'm here all weak.

Dad'Scool RHYME 166

Good grades are important,
But being a good person is more importanter.
-Dad Brad

DAD JOKE 166

I told my wife she was drawing her eyebrows too high.

She looked surprised.

It's a beautiful day that just started.
Better roll down the window,
Cause someone farted.
Have a good day, even if it stinks.
There's good out there
It's all in how you think.
Oh, and if the good you don't see
It's up to you to go and be.
-Dad Brad

DAD JOKE 167

What city in Nevada do all dentists like to visit?

Floss Vegas.

Giving is living.
Give more than you take.
For goodness' sake, don't only take.
Be known an as a giver,
Also, give yourself a break,
You're not perfect but please
Give more than you take.
You can have your cake and eat it, too.
Sharing it with others is the coolest thing to do.
-Dad Brad

DAD JOKE 168

What do you call a man with a rubber toe?

Roberto.

Don't interrupt.
Let someone finish talking.
Despite if you think the
Conversation is lacking.
Wait until it's your turn
Or just listen and see what
You can learn.
-Dad Brad

DAD JOKE 169

What's the name of the guy that can't stand?

Neil.

Dad'Scool RHYME 170

Remember who you are.
In my eyes, you're a star.
In life, you'll go far
If you believe in who you are.
-Dad Brad

DAD JOKE 170

How do you make a tissue dance?

You put a little boogie on it.

Don't be too hard on others or yourself
You'll make mistakes; you'll need help.
Lend a helping hand rather than judge.
When you feel helpless, like you can't budge,
There's a law in life, called Karma.
You get what you serve. You get what you give.
The good side of Karma is a great way to live.
-Dad Brad

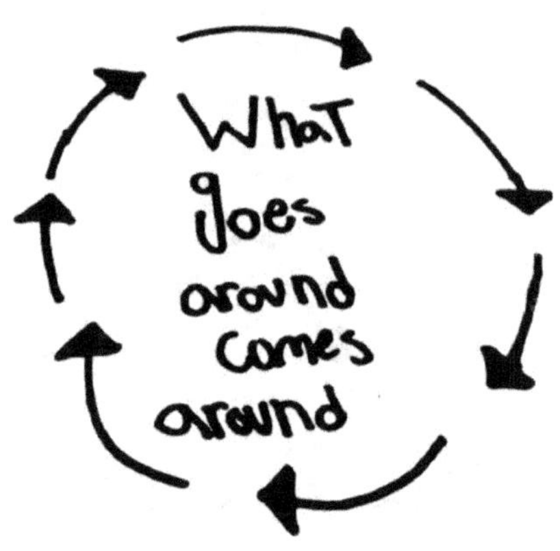

DAD JOKE 171

What kind of cheese is good, but isn't yours?

Nacho Cheese.

Dad'Scool RHYME 172

You'll make mistakes, all people do.
It's how you handle them that defines you.
Learn, and move on; that's the best thing to do.
-Dad Brad

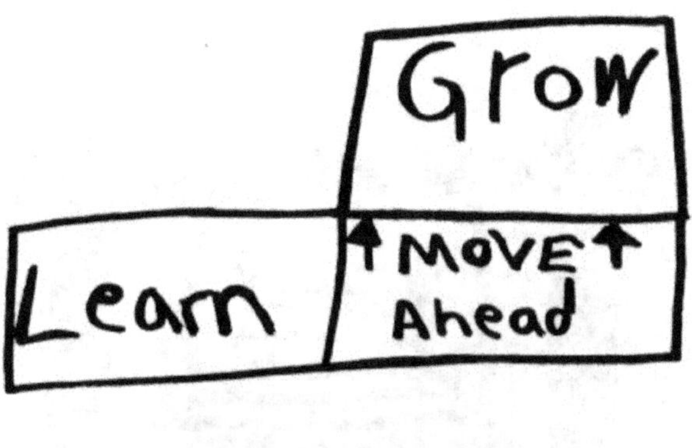

DAD JOKE 172

I wouldn't buy anything that is made with Velcro.

It's a total rip off.

Dad'Scool RHYME 173

Little moments are what makes a good life.
The porch swing, the popsicle on a summer night.
The favorite song, a pretty girl or cute guy you like.
Spending time with loved ones,
Being in the moment, leads to a good life.
-Dad Brad

DAD JOKE 173

What happened when the frog's car died?

He needed a jump; it didn't work so he had to get it toad.

Dad'scool RHYME 174

My daughter, my son.
Your shine outshines the shiniest morning sun.
The moment you were born, you touched my heart.
Seeing you smile, hearing your laugh, I fall apart.
As your dad, I'll make lots of mistakes,
But I'll do whatever it takes,
To make the world sounder and safe.
Because someday, your personality, your talents,
Your kindness will blow us all away.
I can't wait for that day.
P.S.
This rhyme is inspired by the Hamilton play,
That you and mom sing to each day.
-Dad Brad

DAD JOKE 174

How many apples grow on a tree?

All of them.

Dad'scool RHYME 175

Kids, remember this please,
You are the Bees Knees.
It's a phrase that dates back to the 1920's.
It's fun to say and sounds kinda funny.
It's an outstanding person or thing,
Which is you, so continue to bring,
Your uniqueness, your gifts
The thing that makes you be,
The outstanding person, who is the Bees Knees.
-Dad Brad

DAD JOKE 175

Do you think February can March?

I don't know, but April May.

There is opposition in everything.
Here's what I mean:
The word Hurt has four letters and so does Heal.
Anger has five and so does Happy.
Enemies has seven and so does Friends.
Negative has eight and so does Positive.
This means we choose how we live.
We decide how much attention we give,
To the bad side or the good side.
Focus more on the good to have a great life.
-Dad Brad

DAD JOKE 176

The cashier at the grocery store asked if
my dad wanted the milk in a bag.

My dad said, "No, just keep in in the carton."

In school, your teacher gives a lesson
where you'll try your best on the test
To score higher than the rest.
Well, in life there is much more
Then scoring the best score.
In life you'll be given a test.
One you probably haven't studied for
And at times feel you can't endure
But it's in the test where you're taught a lesson
One that'll help with your ultimate progression.
-Dad Brad

DAD JOKE 177

My piano teacher said the goal is to learn to play by ear.

I'd rather just keep using my hands.

Dad'Scool RHYME 178

Consume good food, conversations, and good media.
Focusing on the negative does no good for ya.
You'll always find whatever you're looking for.
There's plenty of bad but look for good more.
You get what you focus on.
Focus on positive.
It's your life to live; give it your best.
Consume the good and the best you'll get.
-Dad Brad

positively Good

DAD JOKE 178

How do cats end their fights?

They hiss and make up.

Dad'scool RHYME 179

To Rise.
Like a sunrise, you will rise.
No matter the storm in the sky,
The sun doesn't bother; it just opens its eyes.
A new day, new beginning, come what may.
There will be days when you feel lazy, or maybe,
Too discouraged to start again.
These are times when you feel you can't win.
How do you overcome and beat the slump?
When you get knocked down, you get back up.
Be like a sunrise, eyes to the sky.
Always rise.
-Dad Brad

DAD JOKE 179

My wife said to take the spider out
instead of stomping on it.

We went and had some dinner. He
seems nice. He's a web designer.

Dad'Scool RHYME 180

A day will come when Dad's not cool.
He'll cherish the days of Dad'Scool Carpool.
You're going to butt heads; you most certainly will
And hanging with friends will be the biggest deal.
Dad will be around and love you, still.
The time will come when it'll be your turn,
To share with your kids, the lessons you've learned.
Dad will get old and won't always be around.
His body will get weak and buried in the ground.
But you'll always have these times in the car,
Listen closely, he'll never be far.
He's loved this chance to teach you these things.
Watching you share them with your kids,
An eternal happiness, it brings.
Dad loves you, above all things.
-Dad Brad

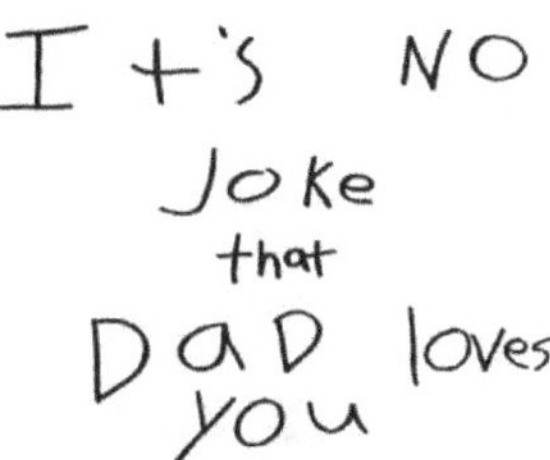

DAD JOKE 180

What did the gardener's toddler say?

I wet my plants.